TE

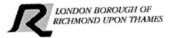

'Robot Rocket' and 'You Are It!'
An original concept by Rebecca Colby
© Rebecca Colby 2022

Illustrated by Gareth Robinson

Published by MAVERICK ARTS PUBLISHING LTD
Studio 11, City Business Centre, 6 Brighton Road,
Horsham, West Sussex, RH13 5BB
© Maverick Arts Publishing Limited May 2022
+44 (0)1403 256941

A CIP catalogue record for this book is available at the British Library.

ISBN 978-1-84886-876-2

www.maverickbooks.co.uk

Red

This book is rated as: Red Band (Guided Reading)
It follows the requirements for Phase 2/3 phonics.
Most words are decodable, and any non-decodable words are familiar,
supported by the context and/or represented in the artwork.

Robot Rocket
and
You Are It!

By Rebecca Colby

Illustrated by
Gareth Robinson

The Letter R

Trace the lower and upper case letter with a finger. Sound out the letter.

Down,
up,
around

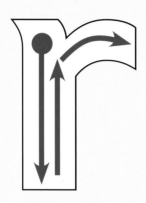

Down,
up,
around,
down

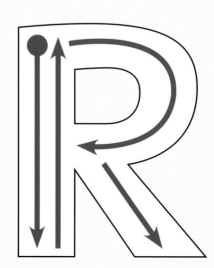

Some words to familiarise:

rocket   wet   dim

High-frequency words:

in   a   the   off   is   it   go

Tips for Reading 'Robot Rocket'

- Practise the words listed above before reading the story.

- If the reader struggles with any of the other words, ask them to look for sounds they know in the word. Encourage them to sound out the words and help them read the words if necessary.

- After reading the story, ask the reader how many planets Tin and Bucket visited.

Fun Activity

Make a rocket from recycled items!

Robot Rocket

Tin and Bucket get in a rocket.

The robots set off!

The robots get in
the rocket and go.

The robots get in the rocket and go.

The robots get in
the rocket and go.

The robots get in the rocket and go.

The Letter Y

Trace the lower and upper case letter with a finger. Sound out the letter.

*Down,
around,
up,
down,
around*

*Down,
lift,
down,
down*

Some words to familiarise:

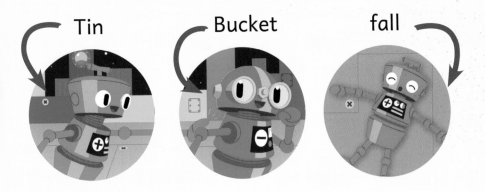

Tin   Bucket   fall

High-frequency words:

to   he   you   are   it   up

Tips for Reading 'You Are It!'

- Practise the words listed above before reading the story.

- If the reader struggles with any of the other words, ask them to look for sounds they know in the word. Encourage them to sound out the words and help them read the words if necessary.

- After reading the story, ask the reader why Tin and Bucket fall down at the end.

Fun Activity

Play a game of tag!

He taps him.

Tag! You are it!

Bucket runs to Tin.

He taps him.

Tin stops. He cannot run.

He falls down.

Bucket runs to Tin.

He picks Tin up.

Tin and Bucket fall down.

Book Bands for Guided Reading

The Institute of Education book banding system is a scale of colours that reflects the various levels of reading difficulty. The bands are assigned by taking into account the content, the language style, the layout and phonics. Word, phrase and sentence level work is also taken into consideration.

Maverick Early Readers are a bright, attractive range of books covering the pink to white bands. All of these books have been book banded for guided reading to the industry standard and edited by a leading educational consultant.

Pink

Red

Yellow

Blue

Green

Orange

Turquoise

Purple

Gold

White

To view the whole Maverick Readers scheme, visit our website at www.maverickearlyreaders.com

Or scan the QR code above to view our scheme instantly!